NAYLAND BLAKE

SOME KIND OF LOVE:

PERFORMANCE VIDEO 1989-2002

IAN BERRY

with an essay by DAVID DEITCHER

THE FRANCES YOUNG TANG TEACHING MUSEUM AND ART GALLERY

AT SKIDMORE COLLEGE

709.0707
B581Be

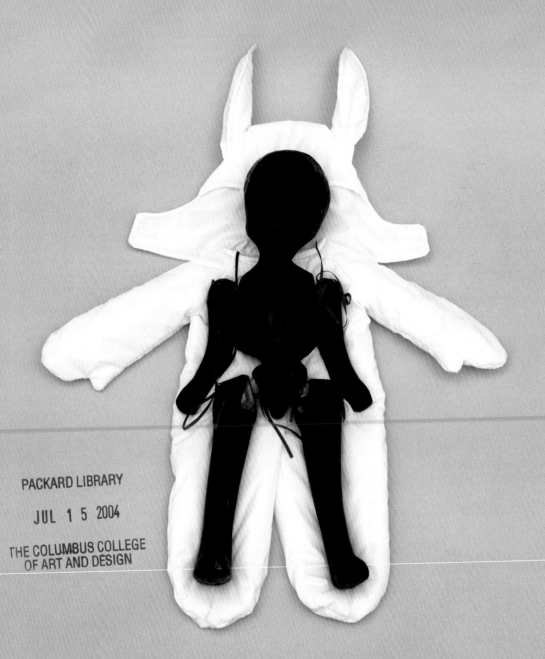

SOME KIND OF LOVE

A Dialogue with NAYLAND BLAKE by Ian Berry

Nayland Blake creates performances, videos, sculptures, and drawings that complicate notions of cultural and sexual identity with disarming humor and intellectual rigor.

Blake's performance-based works are often displayed through video and include works such as *Gorge* where the artist is continuously fed for sixty minutes, or *Starting Over*, in which he tries to perform a simple dance in a tremendously heavy bunny suit. In both, the divide between care and punishment becomes blurred as the intricacies of nurturing, intimacy, and submission are exposed. Author Samuel Delany recently suggested that Blake's work joins a "discourse that may help stabilize an understanding of ways art can fit into the world that have rarely been acknowledged before." Blake's generosity is at the heart of this discourse. He is physically and emotionally bare in his artworks in ways that invite us to consider our own relationships, histories, and pleasures. Through these welcoming provocations, Blake begins a dialogue that sets the stage for self-discovery and transformation.

IAN BERRY Let's start with Joseph Cornell. You cite Cornell as an important influence and continuing presence in your work—someone you once described as "an artist of arrangement rather than invention." Do you define yourself that way as well? What was your first encounter with his work and what are some of the ways he continues to inspire you?

NAYLAND BLAKE The earliest encounter with Cornell I can remember is seeing his 1940 box construction, *Taglioni's Jewel Casket* in the collection of the Museum of Modern Art. I was probably around 8 or 10. My parents would take me to museums fairly often, and it was something that always stayed with me—it's an intimate piece that invites handling. Cornell's pieces are a rebuke to the notion of pure sculpture existing in an abstract realm beyond the viewer's

(title page)
The Little One, 1994
Porcelain and nylon
(shown closed)
26 x 20 x 4.5"
Courtesy of the artist and
Matthew Marks Gallery

(facing page)
The Little One, 1994
Porcelain and nylon
(shown open)
26 x 20 x 4.5"
Courtesy of the artist and
Matthew Marks Gallery

experience of them. They are always conversational objects, and yet his formal arrangements are precise and rich as Dutch still life paintings. But he's a dangerous artist for other artists because the work is so idiosyncratic. He so thoroughly explored the shadow box form; it's virtually impossible for anyone else to attempt it. As soon as you do, it ends up just looking like a weak version of his work. Since much of my work is involved with selection and arrangement, I owe a tremendous debt to him. Even the experience of watching video on a monitor is like looking at a shadow box—colored images behind glass inside a box. It's actually a very Victorian experience.

IB Cornell also made a few sculptures in large glass vitrines, which refer to natural history museums and their displays. There are pieces you have made that resemble these cabinets. Can you talk about natural history dioramas and their influence?

NB It began in my childhood: first, going to the Sinclair oil exhibit at the 1964 World's Fair. Sinclair's logo is a dinosaur, and they had a group of life size animatronic dinosaurs in their pavilion, and Ford had an exhibit nearby that was a march through time. You rode in a Ford car along a conveyor belt and saw several tableaux depicting different moments in history. At that age these experiences got mixed in my mind with visits to the American Museum of Natural History and the New York Aquarium. For years I had dreams of natural history museums and have been fascinated with the displays, the way there are worlds within worlds, somehow both real and artificial. I also respond more to the exhibition strategies in those places, where your surroundings are dark and the thing exhibited is illuminated, instead of the method that has become standard for contemporary art, where everything, viewer and object, is brightly lit.

IB When you started making objects for galleries and museums that used combinations of objects, were you thinking of how reality functions? Are they meant to be pieces of metal and plastic, or a dinosaur and a bunny?

Boredom of the Hyperboreans,
1987
Stereoscope, photo, carpet,
chair, table, tripod
60 x 96 x 26"
Installation view, San Francisco
Camerawork Bookstore

NB At the time I referred to them as props. The objects in my work
are props in the same way that a chair on the stage is functional,
it is something that you can sit on, yet at the same time it is acting
the part of a chair in the play. It's there to give us certain types of
information when we look at it. So it embodies a kind of double
consciousness. We see it both as a particular thing, and also as an
abstraction. That allegorical or emblematic effect continues to be
interesting to me.

The term prop also indicates the way that the pieces leave an opening, either physical or conceptual for the viewer to project themselves into. I hope that they put you as the viewer at center stage.

IB So for example, your vitrines that contain shelves and bunnies made from a combination of materials, they are bunnies but they are also...

NB ...collections of mundane materials. I expect things to read on a number of levels. Actually before the workstation pieces, there were many more vitrine pieces, and I started to get suspicious

Vitrine from
Invisible Man, 1994
Mixed media
Dimensions variable
Installation view,
Baltimore Museum of Art

about the ease with which that strategy worked. I kind of backed off from it for a while, it is seductive, a kind of underlining— everything seems important when it's placed in a vitrine.

IB Everything can become a potent symbol?

NB Everything can seem like that whether or not it actually becomes it. It happens very quickly, and I started to feel it was too simple. These things were becoming art too fast, so I got rid of the vitrine to see if I could make it happen without that kind of underlining.

IB So, you continued to make groupings of objects, but took the box or the frame away. How do you imagine people decipher these works? Do you intend for narratives to be read into your sculpture and videos?

NB I hope that people are willing to give the works time, to allow them to unfold beyond the time that they may actually be looking at them. Of course the viewing of art is a narrative experience. I think the problem arises when we forget this. When I start to read a book I do not expect to already know everything that is in the book before I read it. When I finish it I may not necessarily have gotten everything that is in the book, but months or years down the road I will be reading something else and something will fall into place about what I read before. I am more interested in my work having that kind of resonance for people rather than presenting them with some sort of puzzle that they finish and then throw away. The best games offer a variety of outcomes rather than the same one over and over.

IB I think many viewers in the museum expect to learn a lesson and move on.

NB Yes, I think that there is a tendency towards the rebus, towards visual ideas that involve simple decoding that leave the viewer with a definite solution at the end. Many people are convinced that's what you are supposed to do with a work of art, but it is often those parts of artworks that we cannot resolve that are the most important and the most individual to the artist. I know for me the details that I come back to are the unresolved parts of my pieces. These lead me to the next piece. That is what I am always working towards.

IB Do you think of media in that way also?

NB I think that sometimes I am drawn to material problems, like trying to get a particular material to do something.

IB Do you give yourself tasks or practical problems to solve?

NB I am a big one for assignments. Once I gave myself an assignment to make one piece a day, and for a show in San Francisco I made all stripe paintings, just like classic abstract, stripe paintings. Many of my students were shocked to see those shows. One said to me, "I didn't know that you were allowed to do this". This points to the fact that artists are being trained in schools to limit their thinking, their sense of possibility for what art can be or what it can do. They're encouraged to believe that if you make a certain type of work, performance for example, or "political art" then the next day you couldn't make abstract paintings. Of course those distinctions simply blind us to seeing the ways that painting might function as performance or how identity may be performed through abstraction. Artistic play is an activity that needs rules— that's what makes it satisfying—but some are more useful than others. I think the current rigid categories in the discussion of art are of no benefit to artists.

IB When you are thinking of these projects does the audience ever come into the equation?

NB I make my pieces so that I can see something. The audience that I imagine are the people that I love in terms of their work. Whenever I meet with artists in the studio, I always ask who are you a fan of, who are the people that you love—not necessarily visual artists, but also bands, authors, filmmakers, etc. I try to sneak a look at what cds they have hanging around. Ultimately these are the people that we are making work for. I think more about bands or writers when I am making work than other visual artists, or any fictitious audience.

IB Do you think of them as your sources, as your peers, or as your imagined perfect opening guests where they all come to see your show?

NB All of those. If you hold this group in mind and are lucky, it will actually come to pass. For me, one of my people is the writer, Kathy Acker. I first read her work when I was in college and I thought it was completely right and compelling—nine years later I got to work with her and over time we became friends.

IB What was it about her writing? What do you remember from reading her work?

NB The way she was recycling text and re-writing—using the process of rewriting to make her own voice. The way that much of her writing is retelling stories. I love to read, and her work makes reading a generative, aggressive act. Another figure like that for me is science fiction writer, Samuel Delany. When I read his book, *Dhalgren*, I was in junior high and it was hugely important for me. Almost thirty years later I've had the privilege of showing him what I do.

Nkisi (Saviors), 1997
Mixed media
73 x 12 x 12"
Courtesy of the artist and
Matthew Marks Gallery

IB They form a gang for you.

NB It is also like a jazz model of culture, where people handle ideas and pass them back and forth, where works of art call forth responses in the form of other works. For me, culture is like someone saying "I do it like this" and then someone else says "well I do it like this," and it is those continuing inflections and refractions back and forth where culture lives. It is that constant movement in-between various members of a community. Thinking about your ideal audience in that way keeps you from talking down to them. I have a lot of trouble with the way artists are trained to think about the idea of audience. The suggestion is always that things need to be simplified so that the audience can "get it." I have never heard an artist say "my audience is going to be a lot smarter than I am so I have to really make this piece much smarter because they are really on the ball." Instead there is always this kind of hidden contempt, when you are talking about an audience. It is like we are automatically talking about someone who is not up to speed. I have gained so much from the experiences of having to stretch myself to accommodate an idea that I was unaccustomed to or master a concept that I have not been able to before. I think it is an important part of what making art allows us to do. It's important to come up against your own limitations and to try to move beyond them. It is one of the reasons why I am so attracted to the writings of authors like De Sade. There is an absolute in his writing that I am constantly forced to measure myself against.

IB What do you mean by an absolute?

Still Life, 1989
Sony video 8, shelf
8.5 x 5 x 5"
Collection of Robert Shimshack

NB He was willing to go to places that are difficult to go to, to constantly tangle philosophy and pornography, so that mind and body are inseparable—you cannot divorce the two. De Sade is saying if you remove God from the equation, you cannot then pretend that philosophy issues from anything other than bodies, bodies that also eat, have sex, make waste and are tied to the animal. The extremity of that writing has a value, because it allows you to understand the contours of your own thoughts, the contours of your own body system, because you discover where you will draw the line in relationship to where you find pleasure, or how people should behave in society.

IB Who are other voices that you keep in your gang?

NB Ray Johnson, Sun Ra, and Jack Smith for sure—The Velvet Underground, Djuna Barnes, Ree Morton.

IB Jack Smith's environments and happenings were influential to so many people. People who, whether or not they were actually involved with his events, hold on to a lasting impression of his work, whether they be artists, writers, or from the theater scene.

NB There is an absolute in his work as well—a kind of resistance to success. It is his absence as much as his presence that I think is really important to people. Also, for me starting out, I saw his film *Flaming Creatures* pretty early on, in my high school years. My friends and I were art nerds, and the way that we expressed our nerdiness was through a really obsessive involvement with obscure culture. We went to anthology Film Archives for movies, listened to early Frank Zappa records and drew comics. We hung out in the loft jazz scene in the mid to late 1970s, and went to lots of performances by artists like Richard Foreman.

IB I see Foreman as an important influence on the video pieces you have been making recently. At that time was his work non-linear and chaotic as it is now?

NB Well, I think more multi-valent than chaotic. I saw my first one at 13, a musical, *Dr Salavey's Magic Circus*. I had never seen anything like it. I was totally into it, and I still remember to this day there was a prop that the hero wore near the end. He had been in some sort of an institution, and he was wearing a bowl-like object on his head with stuff dangling from it that looked sort of like dogs ears or shit. A very weird kind of prop—funny, humiliating, and oddly sympathetic at the same time. It's always stuck with me. Every Foreman play I've seen since has had at least one object like that in it. His props are more psychologically acute than most sculpture you see out there.

IB One of your early video pieces *Transport #5* (1990) includes footage from John Carpenter's remake of *The Thing* which focuses on the gory results of an alien infection in one of the characters. A surreal and yet also obviously fake prop is the focus of your chosen frames. Why this segment from this movie? Are you referring us to real infections and some of the gory realities of the 1980s?

NB *The Thing* is a remarkable film because it is impossible to view it now without thinking of AIDS: here's an isolated, exclusively male community, confronted with an alien infection that travels through blood, mimics the host and induces catastrophic bodily breakdown. But the film was made before there was any public discussion of AIDS, indeed before the term was coined or imagined. What this says to me is that the discourses that framed the perception and reaction to AIDS were already in place before the disease was. In fact, they are the discourses that strove to describe homosexuality. If you watch the John Hawks film that Carpenter's is a remake of, you see a similar paranoia played out in cold war terms—where effete scientists are ready to compromise and even capitulate to the alien menace while it is left to the clearly heterosexual men of the army to save civilization.

In my piece I juxtapose a re-edited sequence from the film with an essay from a home-furnishing book from the 1970s, *High Tech*. The essay, by the former design curator for the Museum of Modern

Art, is a hyperbolic argument for the use of functional industrial materials in the home. To me its tone is as overblown as the action from Carpenter's film, and both can be seen as a kind of functionalism run amok. What is more efficiently designed than a virus?

IB How does the piece figure into your early use of video? In this case it seems you are using found material just like you had in your vitrines and other works. What does video offer as a device? It becomes a medium you return to regularly throughout the 1990s—have you changed the way you work with video as you experiment?

NB In most cases I try to think about the sculptural aspects of video. Both *Transport #5* and *Still Life* (1989) are video sculptures, in that the position and appearance of the video apparatus is as important as the image that's on the screen. While that has remained important to me, the more recent pieces are more

Transport #5 (function), 1990
Two Sony monitors, two video
8 players, three steel trolleys
Dimensions variable
Courtesy of the artist and
Matthew Marks Gallery

concerned with video as a recording and experiential medium. For the most part the new pieces are staged records of activities that take place in real time, with no internal edits. These are the sort of formal constraints that are easily legible and hopefully contribute to the immediacy of the piece.

Something struck me as we are talking about the ideal audience: I think this is one of the places where sexuality comes into play, because the societal experience of gay people is one in which they have to be much more aggressive about finding the people they belong with, their tribe. The family is not an automatic substitute for their tribe. When you were talking about a gang, that was very much my experience in high school, I had a gang. Peter Schjeldahl once told a group of my students that they were like a pack. He said, "you are all in a little gang in college, and then you will graduate and you will be in the pack for awhile, and then it will start to disintegrate and you will have to figure out how to get your energy from some place that is not like your pack, because you will have less access to each other." I thought this was an uncommonly astute observation about the artists' life. The experience of consciously seeking out your pack without regret is something that happens more easily for gay people. In our contemporary culture gay people have a leg up on straight people because they have a moment at which they have to declare themselves sexual. Straight people don't have that moment when they announce themselves as sexual beings. I think that is a huge cultural problem. In many other societies there is a moment, there is a specific ritual associated with announcing one's self as a sexual being. The fact that that doesn't really happen in American culture creates a confusing and problematic situation. I think there is something operating in my work that refers to the ways in which sexual subcultures are kind of pedagogic.

IB How they teach themselves?

NB I am interested in how they teach each other about pleasure. This is something that has become more explicit since the advent of AIDS. For example, there is some activity that most people consider outrageous. Delany has written about how the urban environment has been the locus for people's investigation of these behaviors and their dissemination. It was something that people learned to do by seeing other people do it. The rise of group sexual situations in the 1970s really expanded the sexual palette, and is one of the reasons why peers are so important. For me it is like my work and my sexuality are the same thing and function in tandem.

IB How does initiation come into play here?

NB I am intrigued by initiatory cultures. The United States is a broadcast culture, and we are very distrustful of enclaves which we quickly associate with elites. We are in favor of transparency and availability, and these days I am more interested in this sort of initiatory experience, where as in the case with much African art, you do not necessarily get to see the thing. Instead of a cathedral where you take the most important thing, put it at the center, and all lines of sight converge on it. In many African cultures the most important artifact will be hidden from you, will not be visible, and the way that you get access to it is through participating and in the end you may end up seeing something in an obscure way, in dim light, or it might be in motion. If you were able to scrutinize it, it may not look like much—maybe just a rag in a bundle of sticks—but it gained its value through that initiatory process. It gained its value because of what you had to go through to get to it, and I am interested in that model of culture, which in some ways is profoundly anti-democratic.

IB Because it is private...

NB Because it says if everybody has equal access to the thing, then it is sort of gone—its value has disappeared.

IB Is that how it feels for you when you are performing live? Regardless of whether you have the event open to the public or not, it is an experience for a very small number of people— like a moment of exposing that we experience together.

NB In some ways, I think about Jack Smith again. His performance strategy was to winnow down the audience. He wouldn't show up, and if you waited around for four or five hours then maybe the piece would start. At that point you are really dealing with a thing that has gained its value because of your commitment to it. As an audience member, it is opposite to the part of our culture that has embraced a kind of market capitalism that more is better—in this case the fewer the more intimate the better.

IB *Gorge* (1998) records a performance that blurs the divide between care and punishment. As we watch you being continuously fed for sixty minutes on the monitor, the smell of gingerbread from the work *Feeder* (1998) is inescapable. Other artworks in this suite include an image on canvas and a six-pack of Brer Rabbit molasses. Can you describe some of the literary sources that inform these works?

NB The most obvious source for the gingerbread house is the story *Hansel and Gretel*, a story about the uneasy relationship between parents and children revolving around various images of eating and food that is either scarce of too abundant. In the video piece, I was struck by the fact that as much as we eat in the company of others, we never really watch someone else eat. For me the cabin is the archetypical solitary American house, the antithesis of the social town house. Molasses is used to make gingerbread, and the idea of buying it by the six-pack rhymes with the surfeit of food and drink in the video.

IB In the video, you are shown with a friend who is visibly black, and you are legally black but visibly white. Can you talk about that relationship in the piece?

NB Well this is the crux of this country's problem with race at this point, that it is inextricably entangled with representation. Since the notion of race itself is a fantasy, a fabrication that has become a historical horror, those of us who want to rethink it have to come up against the visual: we are trained to scan for signs or visible racial difference in the same way that the British index class status via accent. *Gorge*, in effect is asking "what are you looking at?" and the emotional valences of that answer shift from moment to moment in the tape: nourishment, servitude, submission, play, sex, aggression, pain. From a legal point of view you are watching two African-American men. What does it mean to say that? We have to get to the point where we can experience race as one valence among many, but we can't do that as long as the racial image remains the trump card of interaction, as long as we are made to "represent" race.

IB Your ex-partner, Phillip Horvitz, figures as a central character in *Starting Over* (2000). Even though we never see him, we hear him directing your actions on stage—in addition his body weight determined the amount of beans sewn into your costume. The piece could be read as a portrait of that relationship.

NB I was thinking about how rare it is that contemporary art explores the idea of couple-hood and trying to find a visual equivalent for that. In the piece, Phillip is structuring my actions in two ways: first by choreographing a dance for me to learn and teaching it to me and secondly, by contributing his weight in the form of the suit. So in some ways the visual aspect of the piece is one representation of our relationship and the audio provides another. The piece is built on cooperation, conflict, and the kind of push and pull that we experience daily in relationships.

IB Back to ritual and initiation. In your most recent large-scale work *Coat* (2001), you collaborated with Canadian artist AA Bronson to act out a literal passing on of artistic and sexual knowledge. Could you describe your collaboration?

NB A curator invited us to collaborate. While AA and I knew each other we weren't necessarily close, so the piece is a record of the way we developed an intimacy with each other. AA is much more adept at collaboration than I am, and I think he gave me a great deal of leeway in suggesting options for the piece. I think that in contemporary society we have divorced ritual from the sacred for the most part. So we are left with vestigial habits, or accretions of social activity, that exert an attraction for us but lack the framework to allow us to contemplate their deeper implications. To make this piece was to attempt to find an action that would have some meaningful implications for us, but I don't think that it should be seen as a restoration of a cultural ritual dimension. I'm interested in the initiatory aspects of the piece.

IB Music pervades and can define much of our lives. Was it hard to reveal, let go, and give up such an intimate part of your life by including your entire record collection in your installation, *Ruins of a Sensibility* (2002)?

NB I'm part of a generation that never had to work to encounter popular music, in fact it pours in on us nonstop. *Ruins of a Sensibility* is more about the act of record collecting, and the DJ as curator than it is about music per se. In high school I began to see how record collections functioned for me and my friends as emblems of particular attitudes towards society and culture. It was one of the last instances of "underground culture" in the US. I remember what it meant to hear and see my first punk singles. To possess those things was to belong to a kind of secret club. Today any sort of underground culture is locked in a doomed battle with today's technologies of ubiquity. So the sensibility that is in ruins in the piece is the one that was attached to the collecting and display of those objects. Once I realized that the displaying of all those records had become a personal burden I was free to let them go. The piece is also very influenced by Claes Oldenburgs's *Mouse Museum and Ray Gun Wing*—a piece that I've never really talked about but which I've adored since the first time I saw it. That piece is a walk through the artist's mind. The show "Something Anything," which I curated in 2002 is also an homage to it.

IB *Ruins of a Sensibility* also includes a painting by you and your father, made when you were young. Is this piece also suggesting a rite of passage?

NB The making of that painting is literally one of my first memories, and that painting has hung in my parents living room since the day it was made. It is emblematic of my fondest feelings for my father, and also some of the things that I find hardest to ask him. It was a moment where we shared the making of art, something that I went on to do and which he has stopped doing. So that painting is one of the building blocks of my way of thinking about art, and is also bound up in the various dynamics with my family. I don't know if that implies a rite of passage so much as a kind of degree zero beyond which I cannot pass.

Ruins of a Sensibility
1972–2002, 2002
DJ equipment, records, wood, cardboard boxes, painting
Dimensions variable
Installation view, *Something, Anything*, Matthew Marks Gallery, New York, 2002

Magic, 1990
Puppet, steel, wood, artificial flowers, case
30 x 48 x 24"
Collection of Matthew Marks, New York

The Philosopher's Suite, 1994 (detail)
Mixed media
Dimensions variable
Installation view, Thread Waxing
Space, New York, 1994

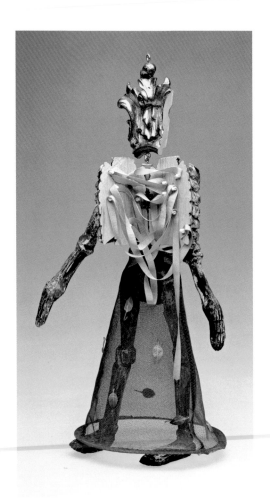

(above left)
Ethyl Eichelberger as Madame de St. Ange, 1991
Painted wood, gold leaf, cloth and metal
23 x 8 x 11"
Private collection

(above right)
Hans Bellmer as Monsieur Dolmance, 1991–93
Wood, cloth and metal
73 x 14 x 12"
Courtesy of the artist and
Matthew Marks Gallery

(facing page)
Joe Dallesandro as Augustin, 1991–94
Painted wood, cloth and metal
73 x 14 x 12"
Courtesy of the artist and
Matthew Marks Gallery

Pierre Molinier as Eugenie, 1991
Painted wood, plastic, cloth and metal
23 x 8 x 11"
Private collection

(facing page)
*The Tabletop Production of Philosophy
in the Bedroom*, 1991–93
Paper, aluminum, steel, wood, plastic
61.5 x 29 x 31"
Courtesy of the artist and
Matthew Marks Gallery

(facing page)
Bleep Crash, 1992
Mixed media
Dimensions variable
Courtesy of the artist and
Matthew Marks Gallery

Controversy 1972–1977–1982, 1993
Mixed media
30.5 x 65.5 x 9"
Courtesy of the artist and
Matthew Marks Gallery

Some kinds of love
Marguerita told Tom
Between thought and expression lies a lifetime
Situations arise because of the weather
and no kinds of love
are better than others

Some kinds of love
Marguerita told Tom
like a dirty French novel
the absurd courts the vulgar
and some kinds of love
the possibilites are endless
and for me to miss one
would seem to be groundless

I heard what you said
Marguerita told Tom
And of course you're a bore
But at that you're not charmless
for a bore is a straight line
that finds a wealth in division
and some kinds of love
are mistaken for vision

Put jelly on your shoulder
Let us do what you fear most
That from which you recoil
but which still makes your eyes moist

Put jelly on your shoulder
lie down upon the carpet
between thought and expression
let us now kiss the culprit

I don't know just what it's all about
Put on your red pajamas and find out.

—Lou Reed

Still from *Negative Bunny*, 1994
Video transferred to DVD with sound, monitor
30 minutes
Courtesy of the artist and Matthew Marks Gallery

Untitled, 1993
Nylon, steel
78.5 x 25 x 14"
Collection of Des Moines Art Center

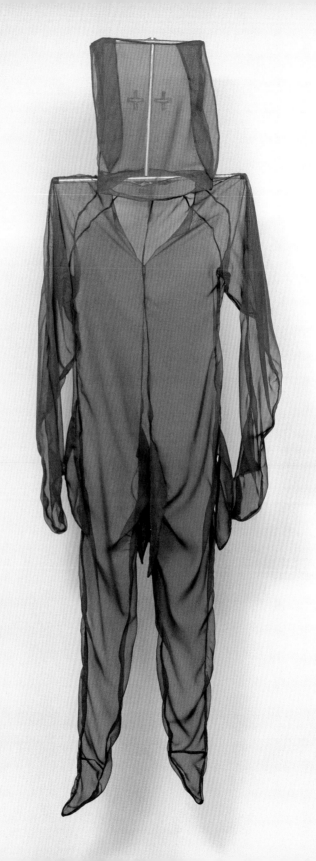

(facing page)
Equipment for a Shameful Epic, 1993
Mixed media
84 x 63 x 32"
Courtesy of the artist and
Matthew Marks Gallery

Stills from *Ghost Bunny,* 1995
Video
30 minutes
Courtesy of the artist and
Matthew Marks Gallery

Surrogates (Bowli), 1994/97
Chocolate, coffee, graveyard dirt,
strychnine, costume jewelry,
handkerchiefs, candy, wax,
rabbits' feet and two glass vitrines
Ten parts, 9.5 x 9 x 2.5" each
Courtesy of the artist and
Matthew Marks Gallery

Bunny Group, Savory Truffle, 1996–97
Graphite and colored pencil on paper
Six sheets, 12 x 9" each
Courtesy of the artist and
Matthew Marks Gallery

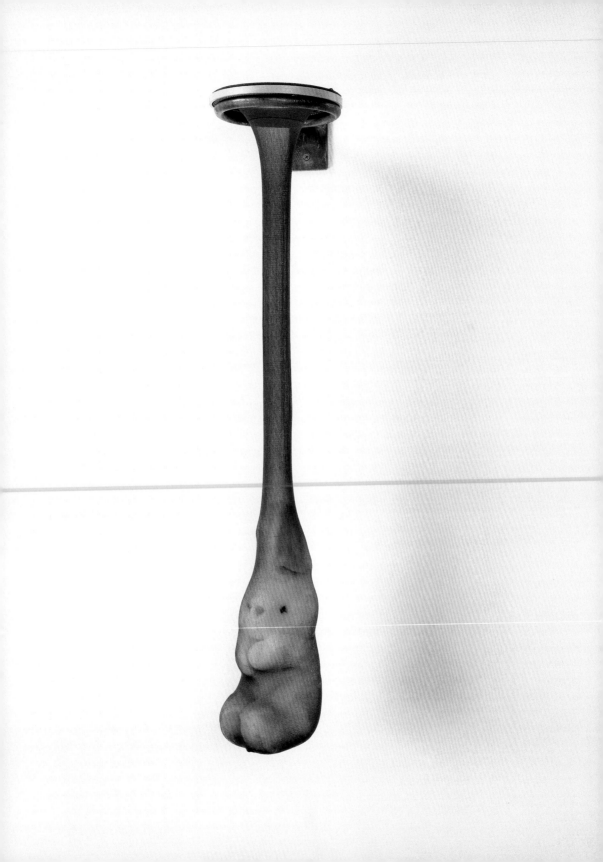

(facing page)
Bunnyhole II, 1997
Steel, nylon, wood and stuffed animal
40 x 7 x 8.5"
Courtesy of the artist and
Matthew Marks Gallery

Bunny Group, After the Turner Diaries,
1996–97
Graphite and colored pencil on paper
Five sheets, 12 x 9" each
Courtesy of the artist and
Matthew Marks Gallery

(overleaf)
Untitled, Pinocchio, 1994
Painted wood
11 x 32 x 4.5"
Private collection, courtesy of
Matthew Marks Gallery

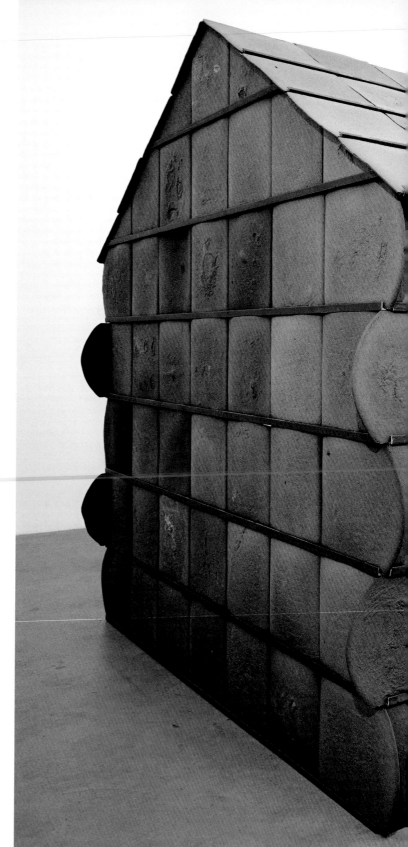

Feeder 2, 1998
Steel and gingerbread
7 x 10 x 7 feet
Collections of Eileen Harris-Norton
and Peter Norton, Santa Monica
Installation view, *Feeder 2 and
Corollary*, Matthew Marks Gallery,
New York, 1998

NAYLAND BLAKE'S FEEDER 2 AND COROLLARY

by David Deitcher

The smell of gingerbread, at once spicy and sweet, conjures similarly pungent childhood memories: of gingerbread cookies and gingerbread houses, and also of one of the more gruesome tales by the Brothers Grimm in which such a house famously appears. These thoughts are occasioned after having visited Nayland Blake's installation *Feeder 2* and *Corollary*, the first impression of which was not visual but olfactory.

Since the late '80s, Blake's sculptural installations and performances have revealed a wide range of interests, from popular culture to vanguard subversion; from Camp to the queer body in the age of AIDS; from Sadean and psychoanalytic texts to the toxic legacy of American racism. In 1995, he co-curated the landmark exhibition, *In a Different Light*, which simultaneously explored, expanded upon, and problematized fundamental assumptions regarding the relationship between queer identity and vanguard culture. Like so many American artists whose work has emerged during the past decade, Blake's projects have often dealt with identity, which they envision as a compound process rather than a *fait accompli*. In his most recent multi-media installation, Blake gave poetic form to such concerns, which is to say that *Feeder 2* and *Corollary* also managed to facilitate identification across lines of difference.

One aspect of the installation that encouraged such identification was the first to strike the viewer upon entering the gallery. The smell of gingerbread pervaded the space of the gallery that housed Blake's exhibtion, and it was only after following the scent that the startling source of the aroma became visible: *Feeder 2*, a lifesize (7 by 10 by 7-foot) cabin made entirely of gingerbread tiles over an armature of steel. Visitors circled the gingerbread house and ducked into its open doorway or windows to see what it was like inside. Some, their hunger awakened by the rich, tangy smell, took to nibbling on it.

Cold Cabin, 1998
Iris print on canvas
15 x 19"
Courtesy of the artist and
Matthew Marks Gallery

This process of at first sensing and then discovering *Feeder 2* effected a kind of bewitchment—precisely the kind of sensual enchantment that lured Hansel and Gretel into the lair of the wicked and hungry witch. It therefore made narrative sense—of a kind that Antonin Artaud as much as the Brothers Grimm would have appreciated—that the smaller adjoining gallery contained objects (the "corollary" noted in the installation's title) that functioned as astringent correctives to the sentimental sense memories aroused by the first gallery's gingerbread house. To be sure, it included a pair of distinctly innocuous white paintings (actually Iris prints on canvas) depicting a snowbound cozy cabin on opposing walls of the gallery, while a third wall (opposite the entrance to this modest space) contained a wall-mounted six-pack of "Brer Rabbit"-brand molasses—this last a reference to a key ingredient in recipes for gingerbread, to a key character in the racially tainted "Uncle Remus" tales of the "Old Plantation" by American author Joel Chandler Harris (1848–1908), and to the many representations of bunnies that have so often and sometimes so cryptically domi-

Stills from *Gorge*, 1998
Video transferred to DVD
with sound, monitor
60 minutes
Courtesy of the artist and
Matthew Marks Gallery

nated Blake's art of the past several years. Notwithstanding these supplemental links to the first gallery's gingerbread house, it was the hour-long video, *Gorge*, playing continuously on a monitor near the entrance to the second gallery, that decisively cut the sweetness to add a different kind of bite to the installation.

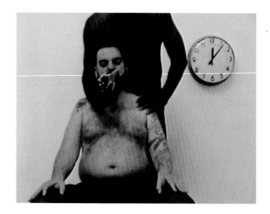
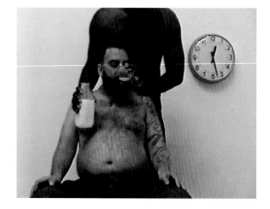

Gorge is in the tradition of the self-punishing, endurance spectacles that established the young Chris Burden as a significant American artist during the early 1970s. Blake's video builds upon this tradition in such a way as to accommodate such issues as the social construction of identity and the latter's personal and political consequences. Throughout *Gorge*, the artist—a decidedly large man—sits naked to the waist, facing the camera in a shallow, brightly lit studio space. Standing nearby is a similarly large and shirtless African-American man. For the better part of the hour, this man feeds Blake: first doughnuts, then pizza, then an enormous "hero" sandwich (which he holds, suggestively, at crotch level like a giant phallus); then watermelon, more pizza, then chocolates. Every so often, the attendant switches from solids to liquids: a half-litre of Perrier water, a quart of milk—all accompanied by the relentlessly upbeat sounds of the "Bunny Hop," a recording of which echoes somewhere in the background.

Because Blake's skin is so much lighter than that of the man who attends to his apparently insatiable appetite, the relationship between the two initially suggests the master/slave dynamic in which—consistent with American history and tradition—it is the black man who serves the white man. But there are complications in what transpires between the video's protagonists that effectively undermine the assumption that power resides chiefly with Blake.

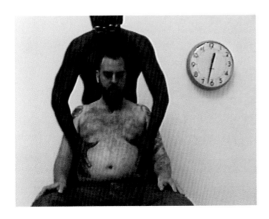 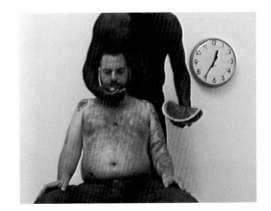

This is not, however, to say that *Gorge* is primarily concerned with the idea that the master's power cannot be absolute because of its dependence upon the existence of the slave. A different kind of dynamic unfolds in *Gorge*, one that generates other ideas and emotions. When, for example, the attendant moves—as he does on several occasions—from a position beside Blake to feeding him from behind, it becomes clear that he is doing something other than just serving him. At such times the attendant has the power not just to deprive Blake of the food he might want, but to administer it more rapidly than he might like.

In fact, *Gorge* reaches a climax of sorts as the attendant tears meat from a watermelon and feeds these dripping chunks to Blake with what to this observer seemed unusual force, ending the sequence by pouring the juice of the spent watermelon onto the artist's chest. That said, I find it difficult to decide how much of this aggression I imagined as a result of the volatile racial charge that is implicit in the spectacle of an African-American man feeding watermelon—whether forcefully or not—to a lighter-skinned man. Consider, in this regard, the use of watermelon as a racist prop by off-duty New York City firefighters and cops who wore blackface and donned Afro wigs to ride through the streets of Queens on a float in a Labor Day parade in September 1998. As if this were not sufficient proof of their racist gambit, they also hung an effigy of a black man off the back of their float in an unmistakable reference to the fate of James Byrd, Jr.—the 49 year old African-American whom white supremacists in Texas murdered on June 7, 1998 by slitting his throat and then by dragging him behind their pickup truck until Byrd's body broke apart.

Even at its most aggressive, however, *Gorge* is not about black rage. In fact, the attendant's actions are more clearly, and more frequently, marked by care than control or cruelty. This is evident as he calibrates the pace of feeding to coincide with Blake's rate of intake; or as he towels food off of the artist's beard and chest, or supportively cradles the back of his head, or rests a hand upon his shoulder. And when, late in the video, he massages Blake's chest and distended belly, it seems a compassionate (if not, finally, a very helpful) thing to do, given the artist's palpable exhaustion and discomfort. In such ways the social relation in *Gorge* goes well beyond describing shifting balances of power to embody a kind of sympathetic ritual. In contrast with recent works by other contemporary artists that allude variously to eating disorders, the compulsive eating in *Gorge* is only one element in a two-part labor that sustains a troubled, empathetic, and sometimes deeply erotic relationship between its two actors. In this way *Gorge* ultimately gives allegorical shape to the unappeasable guilt of the white man—or in Blake's case, to the potentially even greater guilt of the light skinned bi-racial man who can "pass" as white.

In order to walk away from *Gorge* and the other objects comprising the installation's second space, it is necessary to retrace one's steps past the gingerbread house, whose once intoxicating aroma now induces something more like nausea. Such is the dis-illusion caused by experiencing *Gorge* that it effects a lasting ambivalence regarding the object initially perceived as wholly pleasurable—ambivalence being the inevitable result of subjecting even the most bewitching memories (and even the most beautiful works of art) to the rigors of personal and political reflection.

One of the strengths of *Feeder 2* and *Corollary* was the way its disparate elements ultimately came together with the depth and communicative force of a poetic condensation. As Blake's projects have ranged across the artist's extensive and sometimes recondite interests, his iconography has sometimes seemed shrouded in mystery—nowhere more so than in his longstanding use of the rabbit as protagonist, surrogate and alter ego. For when confronted by the spectacle of the artist in a bunny suit, or by the suit hanging by itself in space, or by a wall of pencil drawings featuring an array of rabbits, the viewer's mind races from the Easter Bunny to Bugs Bunny to Brer Rabbit to the rabbit as fertility symbol to Jimmy Stewart's Harvey to one of Joseph Beuys's or Dieter Roth's or Ray Johnson's, hares. In his recent installation, Blake effectively used theatrical, sensory, and narrative devices to narrow his frame of reference. In doing so he brought into greater focus his critical process of self-exploration and poetic experimentation.

Starting Over Suit, 2000
Cloth with 140 pounds of beans,
steel armature
83 x 46 x 22"
Courtesy of the artist and
Matthew Marks Gallery

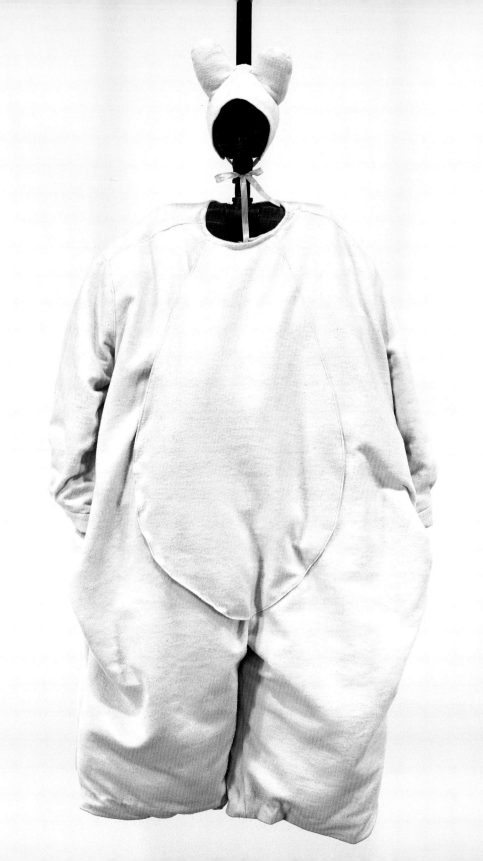

Stills from *Starting Over*, 2000
Video projection with sound, wood
23 minutes
Courtesy of the artist and
Matthew Marks Gallery

Starting Over, 2000
Installation view, Tang Museum,
Skidmore College

1619, Virginia (Liminal), 1997
Mixed media
Dimensions variable
Courtesy of the artist and
Matthew Marks Gallery

(facing page)
Wrong Banyan (After P.), 2000
Aluminum, wood, cotton batting, steel,
artificial tree, fabric, closed circuit television
Dimensions variable
Courtesy of the artist and
Gallery Paule Anglim, San Francisco

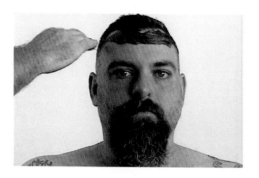 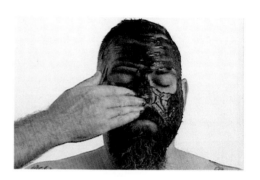

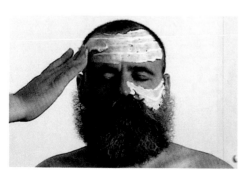 

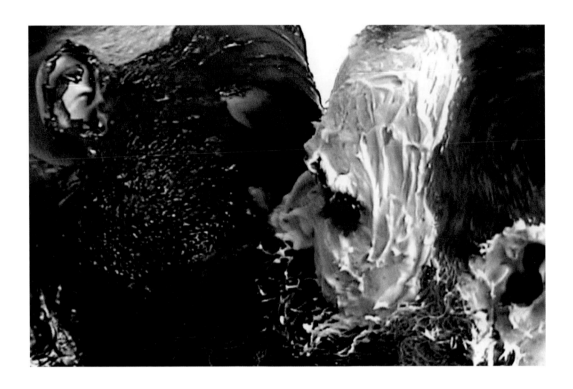

(facing page, detail above)
Nayland Blake and AA Bronson
Stills from *Coat*, 2001
Three DVDs, with sound
Seven minutes each
Courtesy of the artists and
Matthew Marks Gallery

(overleaf)
Ruins of a Sensibility 1972–2002, 2002
DJ equipment, records, wood, cardboard
boxes, painting
Dimensions variable
Installation view, *Something, Anything*,
Matthew Marks Gallery, New York, 2002
Courtesy of the artist and
Matthew Marks Gallery

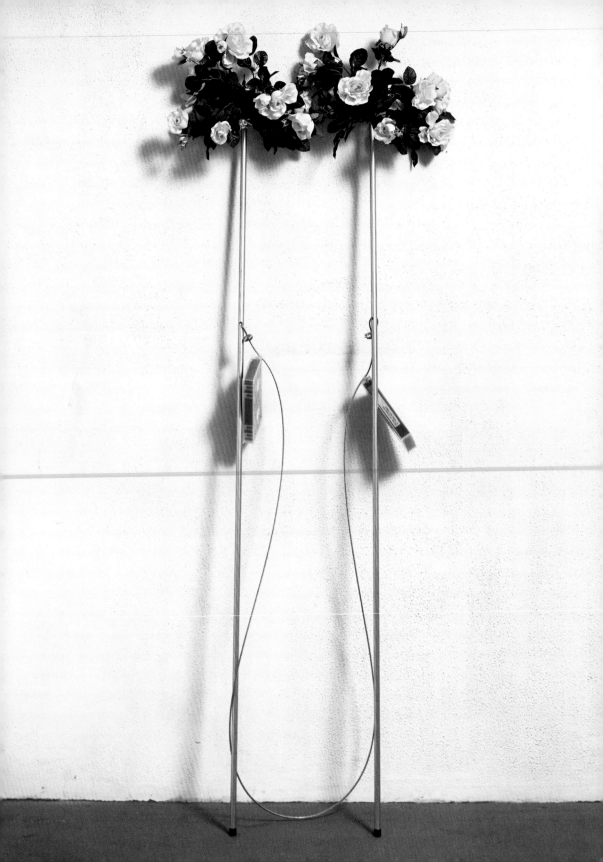

CHECKLIST

All works by Nayland Blake, courtesy of the artist and Matthew Marks Gallery unless otherwise noted; all dimensions in inches, h x w x d

1. *Still Life*, 1989–1990
Video transferred to DVD, portable DVD player, shelf

2. *Magic*, 1990
Puppet, steel, wood, artificial flowers, case
Collection of Matthew Marks, New York

3. *Transport #5 (function)*, 1990
Two videos transferred to DVD, two DVD players, two monitors, three steel trolleys
Dimensions variable

4. *Negative Bunny*, 1993
Video transferred to DVD with sound, monitor
30 minutes

5. *Molasses Six-Pack*, 1998
Molasses, glass bottles, plastic holder
6.75 x 7.75 x 5.25

6. *Cold Cabin*, 1998
Iris print on canvas
15 x 19

7. *Gorge*, 1998
Video transferred to DVD with sound, monitor
60 minutes

8. *Feeder 2*, 1998
Gingerbread, steel
84 x 120 x 84
Collections of Eileen Harris-Norton and Peter Norton, Santa Monica

9. *Starting Over Suit*, 2000
Cloth with 140 pounds of beans, steel armature
83 x 46 x 22

10. *Starting Over*, 2000
Video transferred to DVD with sound, projection, wooden stage
23 minutes, installation dimensions variable

11. *Wrong Banyan (After P.)*, 2000
Aluminum, wood, cotton batting, steel, artificial tree, fabric, closed circuit television
Dimensions variable
Courtesy of the artist and Gallery Paule Anglim, San Francisco

12. Nayland Blake and AA Bronson
Coat, 2001
Three DVDs with sound
Seven minutes each

13. *Ruins of a Sensibility 1972–2002*, 2002
DJ equipment, records, wood, cardboard boxes, painting
Dimensions variable
(Tang Museum only)

(facing page)
Double Feature Standards, 1991
Silk flowers, video cassettes, aluminum, rubber, steel
81 x 34 x 11"
Courtesy of the artist and Matthew Marks Gallery

Molasses Six–Pack, 1998
Six glass bottles of molasses with plastic holder
6.75 x 7.75 x 5.25"
Courtesy of the artist and Matthew Marks Gallery

NAYLAND BLAKE

Born in New York, New York in 1960
Lives and works in Brooklyn, New York

Education

1984

M.F.A., California Institute of the Arts, Valencia, California

1982

B.A., Bard College, Annandale-On-Hudson, New York

Solo Exhibitions

*(Exhibitions are followed by dates where available.
Traveling exhibitions are listed under their initial
date and venue)*

2004

Reel Around, Matthew Marks Gallery, New York, January 16–February 21

2003

Swag, Rhodes and Mann Gallery, London, September 19–November 2
Nayland Blake: Some Kind of Love, Performance Video 1989-2002, Center
    for Art and Visual Culture, University of Maryland, Baltimore County,
    Baltimore, Maryland, February 6–March 22; Tang Teaching Museum
    and Art Gallery at Skidmore College, Saratoga Springs, New York,
    October 18, 2003–January 4, 2004

2000

Nayland Blake, Paule Anglim Gallery, San Francisco, California,
    November 8–December 2
Double Fantasy, Matthew Marks Gallery, New York, April 15–May 26
Nayland Blake, Christopher Grimes Gallery, Santa Monica, California,
    February 25–March 25

1999

Gorge, (three performances), Matthew Marks Gallery, New York
Gorge, (performance) at *Were You There?*, Artis and TU/e, Eindhoven, Netherlands

1998

Feeder 2 and Corollary, Matthew Marks Gallery, New York,
    October 7–November 28

(facing page)
Two Part Self-Portrait, 1996
Color photograph
14 x 12"
Courtesy of the artist

(above)
Family photo, 1966
Color photograph
6.5 x 6.5"
Courtesy of the artist

The Philosopher's Suite, 1994
Mixed media
Dimensions variable
Installation view,
Thread Waxing Space,
New York, 1994

1997

Hare Follies, (Performance), Brooklyn Academy of Music, Artists in Action,
　　Brooklyn, New York, October 23–October 25
April Hare, Paule Anglim Gallery, San Francisco, California, April 2–April 26
The Black/White Album, Matthew Marks Gallery, New York, March 29–April 26

1996

Hare Hole, Christopher Grimes Gallery, Santa Monica, California, May 4–June 1
Nayland Blake: Hare Attitudes, Contemporary Arts Museum, Houston, Texas,
　　January 12–February 25

1995

Jack Hanley Gallery, San Francisco, California, March 30–April 29
Video, Matthew Marks Gallery, New York, February 1–March 11

1994

El Dorado, Christopher Grimes Gallery, Santa Monica, California,
　　October 22–November 26

1993

Jack Hanley Gallery, San Francisco, California, June 3–July 3

Stoney End, Matthew Marks Gallery, New York, March 11–April 24

The Philosopher's Suite, San Francisco Artspace, San Francisco, California, January 12–February 20; Thread Waxing Space, New York, 1994

1992

Mincher/Wilcox Gallery, San Francisco, California

Residency and Exhibition, Milch Foundation, London, England; Galerie Xavier Hufkens, Brussels, Belgium

1990

Low: Good and Evil in the Work of Nayland Blake, Petersburg Gallery, New York, October 6–November 3

Mincher/Wilcox Gallery, San Francisco, California

Punch Agonistes, Richard Kuhlenschmidt Gallery, Santa Monica, California

1989

Matrix 125: Nayland Blake: The Schreber Suite, Matrix Gallery, University Art Museum, Berkeley, California, March–May

The Elision of Failed Effect, Mincher/Wilcox Gallery, San Francisco, California

Richard Kuhlenschmidt Gallery, Santa Monica, California

1988

From Paths of Pain to Jewels of Glory, Media Gallery, San Francisco, California

1987

Boredom of the Hyperboreans, San Francisco Camerawork Bookstore, San Francisco, California

Inscription, XS Gallery, Western Nevada Community College, Carson City, Nevada; Media Gallery, San Francisco, California

1986

3735 Gallery, San Francisco, California

1985

The New Testament, Book One: Der Spinnen, New Langton Arts, San Francisco, California, July 13–August 17

Untitled, 1990
Polystyrene and wool blankets on wall
65.5 x 131 x 12"
Installation view, San Francisco Museum of Modern Art, 1990

Selected Group Exhibitions

2002

The Garden of Violence, Historiche Museum, Murten, Switzerland

2001

Play's the Thing: Critical and Transgressive Practices in Contemporary Art,
  Whitney Museum of American Art Independent Study Program Exhibition,
  Whitney Museum of American Art at Art Gallery of the Graduate Center, the
  City University of New York, New York, May 25–July 8

Uncommon Threads: Contemporary Artists and Clothing, Herbert F. Johnson
  Museum of Art, Cornell University, Ithaca, New York, March 17–June 17

Drawing, Rhodes & Mann, London, England

2000

Made in California: Art, Image, and Identity, 1900-2000, Section 5, 1980-2000,
  Los Angeles County Museum of Art, Los Angeles, California, October 22,
  2000–February 25, 2001

Bestiary, Armory Center for the Arts, Pasadena, California, July 2–August 27

Do Not Touch: An Exploration of Delicate Obsessions, Consolidated Works,
  Seattle, Washington, January 26–February 27

Fusion, Rhodes & Mann, London, England

1999

Through the Looking Glass, Newhouse Center for Contemporary Art, Snug
  Harbor Cultural Center, Staten Island, New York, April 25–December 19

Food for Thought, New Jersey Center for Visual Arts, Summit, New Jersey

1998

The Theater of Cruelty, Christinerose Gallery, New York

Nayland Blake performing
Hare Follies
Brooklyn Academy of Music,
1997

1997

Scene of the Crime, UCLA Armand Hammer
  Museum of Art, Los Angeles, California, July
  23–October 5

New Work: Drawings Today, San Francisco Museum
  of Modern Art, San Francisco, California

1996

a/drift, Center for Curatorial Studies, Bard College,
  Annandale-on-Hudson, New York, October 20,
  1996–January 5, 1997

Intermission, Basilico Fine Art, New York

1995

In a Different Light: Visual Culture, Sexual Identity, Queer Practice, University Art Museum, Berkeley, California, January 11–April 9

Into a New Museum-Recent Gifts and Acquisitions of Contemporary Art, San Francisco Museum of Modern Art, San Francisco, California

1994

Don't Leave Me This Way: Art in the Age of AIDS, National Gallery of Australia, Canberra, Australia, November 12, 1994–March 5, 1995

Black Male: Representations of Masculinity in Contemporary American Art, Whitney Museum of American Art, New York, November 10, 1994–March 5, 1995

Body and Soul, The Baltimore Museum of Art, Baltimore, Maryland, June 22–October 9

Outside the Frame: Performance and the Object, Cleveland Center for Contemporary Art, Cleveland, Ohio, February 11–May 1; Newhouse Center for Contemporary Art, Snug Harbor Cultural Center, Staten Island, New York, February 26, 1995–June 18, 1995

Feeder, 1990 (in foreground)
Steel cage
84 x 42 x 120"
Installation view, Petersburg Gallery, New York, 1990

1993

Up, Up, (and Away), Here Art, New York, October 30–December 9

Mr. Serling's Neighborhood, Christopher Grimes Gallery, Santa Monica,
    California, July 10–September 4

The Uncanny, Gemeentemuseum Arnhem, Arnhem, The Netherlands,
    June 5–June 26

Building a Collection Part 1: The Department of Contemporary Art, Museum
    of Fine Arts, Boston, Massachusetts, January 28–July 3

I am the Enunciator, Thread Waxing Space, New York

I Love You More Than My Own Death, Venice Biennial, Venice, Italy

Sick Joke, Kiki, San Francisco, California

1992

Effected Desire, The Carnegie Museum of Art, Pittsburgh, Pennsylvania,
    October 3–November 29

Dissent, Difference, and the Body Politic, Portland Art Museum, Portland,
    Oregon, August 20–October 18; Otis Parsons School of Art and Design,
    Los Angeles, California, February 20, 1993–March 25, 1993

The Clinic, Rosamond Felsen Gallery, Los Angeles, California, August 1–
    August 29

Nayland Blake, Richmond Burton, Peter Cain, and Gary Hume, Matthew Marks
    Gallery, New York, July 1–September 30

Gegendarstellung: Ethik und Ästhetik im Zeitalter von AIDS, Kunstverein in
    Hamburg, Hamburg, Germany, May 15–June 21; Kunstmuseum Luzern,
    Luzern, Switzerland, October 2–November 22

Psycho, KunstHall, New York, April 2–May 9

Recent Narrative Sculpture, Milwaukee Art Museum, Milwaukee, Wisconsin,
    March 13–May 10

California: North and South, Aspen Art Museum, Aspen, Colorado, February
    13–April 15

The Auto Erotic Object, Hunter College Art Gallery, New York

Translation, Center for Contemporary Art, Ujazdowski Castle, Warsaw, Poland

Without, The Lab, San Francisco, California

1991

*Residue Politics: Nayland Blake, Jennifer Bolarde, Greg Colson, David Hammons,
    Mike Kelley, Karen Kilimnik, Christian Marclay, Christy Rupp.* Beaver College
    Art Gallery, Glenside, Pennsylvania, November 14–December 20

Third Newport Biennial: Mapping Histories, Newport Harbor Art Museum,
    Newport Beach, California, October 6, 1991–January 5, 1992

The Interrupted Life: On Death and Dying, The New Museum of Contemporary
    Art, New York, September 13–December 29

Just What is It That Makes Today's Homes So Different, So Appealing? The Hyde
    Collection, Glens Falls, New York, September 7–November 17

Erotic Drawings, San Francisco Artspace, San Francisco, California, September
    7–October 31

The Good, the Bad, & the Ugly: Knowledge and Violence in Recent American Art,
   Ezra and Cecile Zilkha Gallery, Center for the Arts, Wesleyan University,
   Middletown, Connecticut, September 3–October 6

Facing the Finish: Some Recent California Art, Santa Barbara Contemporary
   Arts Forum, Santa Barbara, California, June 29–August 17; San Francisco
   Museum of Modern Art, San Francisco, California, September 20–December
   1; Art Center College of Design, Pasadena, California, Spring 1992

Situation: Perspectives on Work by Lesbian and Gay Artists, New Langton Arts,
   San Francisco, California, June 18–July 13

The Library of Babel: Books to Infinity, Hallwalls Contemporary Arts Center,
   Buffalo, New York, April 6–May 31; White Columns Gallery, New York,
   April 6–May 31

1991 Biennial Exhibition, Whitney Museum of American Art, New York,
   April–June 1991

*Toward a New Museum: Recent Acquisitions in Painting and Sculpture,
   1985-1991*, San Francisco Museum of Modern Art, San Francisco,
   California, February 28–May 12

Currents, Institute of Contemporary Art, Boston, Massachusetts, January
   17–March 17

Nayland Blake, Ross Bleckner, Donald Moffet, Simon Watson Gallery, New York

1990

Mind Over Matter: Concept and Object, Whitney Museum of American Art,
   New York, October 3, 1990–January 6, 1991

SECA Award Exhibition, San Francisco Museum of Modern Art, San Francisco,
   California, September 27–November 25

Gingerbread House, 2001
Gingerbread, steel
Dimensions variable
Installation view Ursula
Blickle Stiftung,
Unterowisheim, Germany
(with *Arbeit Macht Frei*, 2000
by AA Bronson)

Stendhal Syndrome: The Cure, Andrea Rosen Gallery, New York, June 29–
    August 4
Nachschub/Supply: The Köln Show, Galeries Daniel Buccholz, Gisela Capitain,
    Tanja Grunert, Max Hetzler, Jablonka, Isabella Kacprzak, Esther Schipper,
    Monika Spruth, Sophia Ungers, Cologne, Germany, April 24–May 26
New Work: A New Generation, San Francisco Museum of Modern Art,
    San Francisco, California, February 22–April 22

1989

Image World: Art and Media Culture, Whitney Museum of American Art,
    New York, November 8, 1989–February 18, 1990
Matrix 132: AIDS Timeline, Matrix Gallery, University Art Museum, Berkeley,
    California, November 1989–January 1990
Bay Area Conceptualism: Two Generations, Hallwalls Contemporary Art Center,
    Buffalo, New York, September 15–November 10
Against Nature: A Group Show of Work by Homosexual Men, LACE (Los Angeles
    Contemporary Exhibitions), Los Angeles, California
Erotophobia, Simon Watson Gallery, New York
The New Narratology: Examining the Narrative in Image-Text Art, Artspace
    Annex, San Francisco, California; Santa Cruz County Art Museum, Santa
    Cruz, California; Miami Center for the Fine Arts, Miami, Florida; Center
    for Contemporary Art, Arlington, Texas
Remainders, White Columns Gallery, New York

1988

Ways in Being Gay: A Gallery Installation, Hallwalls Contemporary Arts Center,
    Buffalo, New York, November 15–December 17
Assemblage '88: The Recontextualized Object, San Francisco Art Institute,
    San Francisco, California, July 13–August 20
Nayland Blake, Liz Larner, Richard Morrison, Charles Ray, 303 Gallery,
    New York, January 22–February 14

1987

Gypsies, Tramps, and Thieves, Works Gallery, San Jose, California, December 11,
    1987–January 9, 1988
Chain Reaction 3, San Francisco Arts Commission Gallery, San Francisco,
    California, November 19, 1987–January 16, 1988
Art Installs, ProArts, Oakland, California
Reconnaissance, Media, San Francisco, California

1986

Artists and Models, LACE Bookstore, Los Angeles, California

Bibliography

Untitled, 1992
Wood, metal, chocolate
dimensions
Installation view, Milch
Foundation, London, 1992

Selected Books and Catalogues

Acker, Kathy. *Bodies of Work: Essays*. London and
New York: Serpent's Tail, 1997.

Acker, Kathy. *Low: Good and Evil in the Work of Nayland
Blake*. Exhibition catalogue. New York: Petersburg
Gallery, 1990.

Alden, Todd. *The Library of Babel*. Exhibition catalogue.
Buffalo, New York: Hallwalls Contemporary Center,
1991.

Armstrong, Richard. *Mind Over Matter: Concept and
Object*. Exhibition catalogue. New York: Whitney
Museum of American Art, 1990.

Armstrong, Richard, et al. *1991 Biennial Exhibition*.
Exhibition catalogue. New York: Whitney Museum
of American Art, 1991.

Arning, Bill. *AA Bronson: Mirror Mirror*. Exhibition catalogue. Cambridge: MIT List Visual Arts Center, 2002.

Assemblage '88: The Recontextualized Object. Exhibition catalogue. San
Francisco, California: Emmanuel Walter and Atholl McBean Galleries,
San Francisco Art Institute, 1988.

Barron, Stephanie. *Made in California: Art, Image, and Identity*. Exhibition
catalogue. Los Angeles, California: Los Angeles County Museum of Art;
Berkeley, California: University of California Press, 2001.

Berry, Ian. *Nayland Blake: Some Kind of Love, Performance Video 1989–2002*.
Exhibition catalogue. Saratoga Springs, New York: Tang Teaching Museum
and Art Gallery at Skidmore College, 2003. Essay by David Deitcher.

Blake, Nayland and Pam Gregg. *Situation: Perspectives on Work by Lesbian
and Gay Artists*. Exhibition catalogue. San Francisco, California: New
Langton Arts, 1991. Essays by Liz Kotz and Richard Meyer.

Cameron, Dan. *Just What Is It That Makes Today's Homes So Different,
So Appealing?* Exhibition catalogue. Glens Falls, New York: The Hyde
Collection, 1991.

Cooper, Dennis and Richard Hawkins. *Against Nature: A Group Show of Work
by Homosexual Men*. Exhibition catalogue. Los Angeles, California: LACE
(Los Angeles Contemporary Exhibitions), 1988.

Decter, Joshua. *a/drift*. Exhibition catalogue. Annandale-on-Hudson, New York:
Center for Curatorial Studies, Bard College, 1997.

Golden, Thelma. *Black Male: Representations of Masculinity in American Art*.
Exhibition catalogue. New York: Whitney Museum of American Art, 1994.
Essays by Elizabeth Alexander, et. al.

Gott, Ted. *Don't Leave Me This Way*. Exhibition catalogue. Canberra, Australia:
National Gallery of Australia; New York: Thames & Hudson, 1994.

Harper, Glenn, ed. *Interventions and Provocations: Conversations on Art, Culture, and Resistance*. Albany, New York: State University of New York Press, 1998. Interview by Anne Barclay Morgan.

Heiferman, Marvin and Lisa Phillips. *Image World: Art and Media Culture*. Exhibition catalogue. New York: Whitney Museum of American Art, 1989.

Isé, Claudine and Mary-Kay Lombino. *Bestiary*. Exhibition catalogue. Pasadena, California: Armory Center for the Arts, 2000.

Kelley, Mike. *The Uncanny*. Exhibition catalogue. Arnhem, the Netherlands: Gemeentemuseum Arnhem, 1993.

Knode, Marilu and Anne Ayres. *Mapping Histories: Third Newport Biennial*. Exhibition catalogue. Newport Beach, California: Newport Harbor Art Museum: 1991.

Leigh, Christian. *Psycho: Inaugural Exhibition*. Exhibition catalogue. New York: The Kunsthall, 1992.

Marincola, Paula. *Residue Politics: Nayland Blake, Jennifer Bolarde, Greg Colson, David Hammons, Mike Kelley, Karen Kilimnik, Christian Marclay, Christy Rupp*. Exhibition catalogue. Glenside, Pennsylvania: Beaver College Art Gallery, 1991 Essay by Germano Celant.

Morin, France. *The Interrupted Life*. Exhibition catalogue. New York: The New Museum of Contemporary Art, 1991.

Nayland Blake: Hare Attitudes. Exhibition catalogue. Houston: Contemporary Arts Museum, 1996.

Ottman, Klaus. *The Good, the Bad, & the Ugly: Knowledge and Violence in Recent American Art*. Exhibition catalogue. Middletown, Connecticut: Ezra and Cecile Zilkha Gallery, Center for the Arts, Wesleyan University, 1991.

Something, Anything, 2002
An exhibition organized
by Nayland Blake
Matthew Marks Gallery,
New York

Play's the Thing: Critical and Transgressive Practices in Contemporary Art.
Exhibition catalogue. New York: Whitney Museum of American Art, 2001.

Rinder, Lawrence. *Matrix 125: Nayland Blake: The Schreber Suite.* Exhibition
brochure. Berkeley, California: Matrix Gallery, University Art Museum,
University of California, Berkeley, 1989.

Rugoff, Ralph. *Scene of the Crime.* Exhibition catalogue. Los Angeles,
California: UCLA Armand Hammer Museum, 1997. Contributions by
Anthony Vidler and Peter Wollen.

Sangster, Gary. *Outside the Frame: Performance and the Object.* Exhibition
catalogue. Cleveland, Ohio: Cleveland Center for Contemporary Art, 1994.

SECA Art Award 1990: Nayland Blake, John Meyer. Exhibition catalogue. San
Francisco: San Francisco Museum of Modern Art, 1990.

*Toward a New Museum: Recent Acquisitions in Painting and Sculpture, 1985–
1991.* Exhibition catalogue. San Francisco: San Francisco Museum of
Modern Art, 1991.

Ulmer, Sean M. *Uncommon Threads: Contemporary Artists and Clothing.*
Exhibition catalogue. Ithaca, New York: Herbert F. Johnson Museum of Art,
Cornell University, 2001.

Watson, Simon and John S. Weber. *Dissent, Difference, and the Body Politic.*
Exhibition catalogue. Portland, Oregon: Portland Museum of Art, 1993.

Selected Articles and Reviews

Abbott, Steve. "Tart Art from a Bad Boy." *The Advocate* 558 (August 28, 1990): 66.

Baker, Kenneth. "Nayland Blake." *San Francisco Chronicle* (November 7, 1989).

Baker, Kenneth. "Nayland Blake." *San Francisco Chronicle* (March 10, 1988).

Baker, Kenneth. "Nayland Blake." *San Francisco Chronicle* (October 20, 1988).

Baron, Todd. "Narratives of Repression." *Artweek* 21 (May 24, 1990): 13.

Berkson, Bill. "San Francisco, Nayland Blake, Media." *Artforum* 25, no. 9
(May 1987): 157.

Bischoff, Dan "A Matter of Taste." *Sunday Star Ledger* (April 4, 1999): 001.

Bollen, Christopher. "Nayland Blake, 'Double Fantasy.'" *Time Out New York*
(May 11–18, 2000): 71.

Bonetti, David. "Pulling the Rabbit Out of the Hat." *San Francisco Examiner*
(December 28, 1992).

Bonetti, David. "Portrait of the Artist as a Dandy." *San Francisco Examiner*
(October 29, 1989): E1, E6.

Brenson, Michael. "In the Arena of the Mind at the Whitney." *The New York
Times* (October 19, 1990): C33.

Breslauer, Jan. "Nayland Blake." *L.A. Weekly* (January 26, 1989).

Brock, Hovey. "Nayland Blake, Richmond Burton, Peter Cain, Gary Hume."
ARTnews 91, no. 9 (November, 1992): 140.

Brunson, Jamie. "Nayland Blake." *Artweek* (April 30, 1988).

Burnham, Scott G. "Resistance, Rebellion and Death." *The Daily Free Press*
(January 24, 1991).

Cameron, Dan. "The Sexual is Cultural." *Art & Auction* (December 1990).

Carr, C. "Bunny Hop." *The Village Voice* (April 25, 2000): 54.

Cohen, Michael. "Review–Nayland Blake." *Flash Art* no. 209 (1999): 115.

Cotter, Holland. *The New York Times* (November 20, 1998).

Cunningham, Michael. "Cookie Monster." *Nest* (Winter 2000).

Curtis, Cathy. "Nayland Blake." *Los Angeles Times* (May 15, 1990).

D'Amato, Brian. "Mind Over Matter." *Flash Art* (January/February 1991).

De Carlo, Tessa. "Puppet Show for Adults Only." *The Wall Street Journal*
      (April 12, 1993): A8.

Decter, Joshua. "Nayland Blake." *Artforum* 33, no. 3 (November 1994): 85.

Faust, Gretchen. "New York in Review: Nayland Blake." *Arts* (March, 1990).

Fehlau, Fred. "Against Nature: Whose Nature?" *Art Issues* (May, 1989).

Fehlau, Fred. "Nayland Blake; Co-Conspirators: Nayland Blake and
      Kathy Acker." *Flash Art* 154 (October 1990): 190.

Gerstler, Amy. "Nayland Blake." *Artscribe* (May, 1989).

Hammer, Jonathan. "Nayland Blake." *Shift* (1987).

Helfand, Glen. "Objects of Desire." *Artweek* 19 (October 29, 1988): 4.

Hirsch, Faye. "Nayland Blake." *Flash Art* 178 (October, 1994): 98.

Hixson, Kathryn. "Nayland Blake." *Arts Magazine* 63, no.7 (March 1989): 106.

Indiana, Gary. "Science Holiday." *The Village Voice* 33, no.11 (March 15, 1988): 90.

Jenkins, Steven. "Rabbit Habit." *Bay Area Reporter* (May 22, 2997).

Kandel, Susan. "Less-Silly Rabbits." *Los Angeles Times* (May 23, 1996): F11.

Kandel, Susan. "Nayland Blake." *Arts Magazine* 65, no. 1 (September 1990):
      108–109.

Killian, K. "The Secret Histories." *Artforum* 33 (February 1995): 23–24.

Knode, Marilu. "Nayland Blake." (Interview) *Journal of Contemporary Art* 5,
      no. 1 (Spring 1992): 16–29.

Mahoney, Robert. "New York in Review: Nayland Blake." *Arts Magazine* 65,
      no. 5 (January, 1991): 102–103.

McCabe, Bret. "Rabbit's Feat." *City Paper* (February 19, 2003): 32.

McNatt, Glenn. "Art Review." *The Baltimore Sun* (March 6, 2003): 1E.

Morgan, Anne Barclay. "Art, Pleasure, and Community: Interview with
      Nayland Blake." *Art Papers* 19, no. 4 (July 1995): 8.

Morgan, Stuart. "Behavior: Nayland Blake Interviewed by Stuart Morgan."
      Frieze (June/July/August 1992).

Morgan, Stuart. "Low: Good and Evil in the Work of Nayland Blake." *Artscribe*
      (January/February 1991).

Morris, Gay. "Nayland Blake." *Art in America* 78, no. 3 (March 1990): 209.

Pagel, David. "Nayland Blake: Props and Phantoms." *Art Issues*
      (September/October 1990): 12–15.

Pinchbeck, Daniel. "Nayland Blake." *The Art Newspaper* 10, no. 85 (October
      1998): 57.

Porges, Maria. "You're History, Pal: Reading Nayland Blake." *Artforum* 29, no. 3
      (November 1990): 119–123.

Princenthal, Nancy. "Nayland Blake at Thread Waxing Space." *Art in America* 82, no. 12 (December 1994): 103.

Rubenstein, Meyer Raphael. "Spotlight: Nayland Blake." *Flash Art* 156 (January/February 1991): 123.

Rush, Michael. "Nayland Blake." *Art in America* 88, no. 9 (September 2000): 148.

Salvioni, Daniela. "Nayland Blake." *Artforum* 36, no. 2 (October 1997): 104–105.

Simon, Joan. "Art for Tomorrow's Archive." *Art in America* 84 (November 1996): 41–43.

Solnit, Rebecca. "Objects of Provocation." *Artweek* 19 (April 23, 1988): 5.

Van Proyen, Mark. "Nayland Blake." *Artweek* (October 8, 1987).

Weir, John. "The Polymorphous Diverse." *Artforum* 31, no. 2 (October 1992): 8–9.

Weissman, Benjamin. "Nayland Blake, Richard Kuhlenschmidt Gallery." *Artforum* 28, no. 1 (September, 1989): 154–155.

Yablonsky, Linda. "Nayland Blake, 'The Black White Album.'" *Time Out New York* (April 17-24, 1997).

Zimmer, William. "A Feast Where Not Everything Looks Good Enough to Eat." *The New York Times* (April 18, 1999).

Selected Writings

Blake, Nayland. *Bay Area Conceptualism: Two Generations*. Exhibition catalogue. Buffalo, New York: Hallwalls Contemporary Arts Center, 1992.

Blake, Nayland. "James Gobel." Exhibition brochure. Los Angeles: UCLA Hammer Museum, 2000.

Blake, Nayland, Lawrence Rinder, and Amy Scholder, eds. *In A Different Light: Visual Culture, Sexual Identity, Queer Practice*. San Francisco: City Lights Books, 1995.

Blake, Nayland. "Ray Johnson." Review. *Artforum* 37, no. 7 (March 1999): 107–108.

Blake, Nayland. "The Art of Matthew Benedict Shroud of Truro." Review. *Artforum* 39, no. 7 (March 2001): 128–133.

Blake, Nayland. "The Message from Atlantis" in *Jack Smith: Flaming Creature: His Amazing Life and Times* Edward G. Leffingwell, Carole Kismeric, and Marvin Heiferman, eds. London and New York: Serpent's Tail with Institute for Contemporary Art, London and P.S.1 Museum, New York, 1997.

Blake, Nayland. "Tom of Finland: An Appreciation" in *Out in Culture: Gay, Lesbian, and Queer Essays on Popular Culture*. Corey K. Creekmur and Alexander Doty, eds. Durham, North Carolina: Duke University Press, 1995.

Blake, Nayland. "Top Ten." *Artforum.* 39, no. 1 (September 2000): 36.

Cooper, Dennis. *Jerk*. San Francisco, California: Artspace Books, 1993. Illustrated by Nayland Blake.

Landau, Emily Fisher, and Elizabeth Sklenar. *Mishoo: Cosmopolitan Cat*. New York: Whitney Museum of American Art, 2000. Illustrated by Nayland Blake.

ACKNOWLEDGEMENTS

Since Nayland Blake's first works in video in the late 1980s he has consistently returned to the medium to record performance works and to expand on his experiments with sculptural objects in gallery and museum spaces. Blake's interest in modes of display became engagingly apparent when walking through the galleries—experiences ranged from pervasive and loud to intimate and soft, and from small and low to the ground to room-filling projections high on the wall.

Before opening at the Tang Museum, *Some Kind of Love* was on view at the Center for Art and Visual Culture at the University of Maryland, Baltimore County. We are grateful to many there for their collaboration and trust. Thanks to Maurice Berger, Symmes Gardner, David Yager, William John Tudor, Janet Magruder, and students; Beatriz Bufrahi, Jen Twig, Geoff Thomas, David Crandall, Michael Prymas, and Justin Plakas. Renee van der Stelt deserves special thanks for her work managing the project in Baltimore including the daunting task of securing a local gingerbread baker. Alfred and Dana Himmelrich, owners of Stone Mill Bakery and baker, Raymond Mikefell, made the gingerbread for the Baltimore venue and Paul Cerrone baked the gingerbread for the Tang Museum venue. The order is an unusual one and involves a generous sense of creativity and collaboration. We are grateful to both.

Special thanks to art historian David Deitcher for his insightful essay, and to designer Bethany Johns who has created another wonderful catalogue for our Opener series with photographs by Arthur Evans and Bill Jacobson among many others.

Matthew Marks and Jeffrey Peabody of Matthew Marks Gallery in New York have been ever-present partners during the organization of all facets of this project. Also thanks to Victoria Cuthbert, Aimee McElroy, Danielle Thornton, and Ryan Hart who have graciously helped along the way. They answered questions, assisted with loans and catalogue details, and provided steady encouragement throughout.

Thanks to the funders of the Opener series, The Laurie Tisch
Sussman Foundation, The New York State Council on the Arts,
the Overbrook Foundation, and the Friends of the Tang.

At the Tang Museum, thanks to installation crew members
Sam Coe, Torrance Fish, Jefferson Nelson, Chris Oliver, Patrick
O'Rourke, Alex Roediger, Thaddeus Smith, and Joe Yetto. Thanks
to Tang staff Tyler Auwarter, Helaina Blume, Jill Cohan, Lori
Geraghty, Elizabeth Karp, Susi Kerr, Gayle King, Chris Kobuskie,
and Barbara Schrade, and Gretchen Wagner. Also thanks to
Barbara Melville, Mary Jo Driscoll, Barry Pritzker, and Elizabeth
Marena for their support, and museum interns Rosie Garschina
'03, Megan Hurst '03, Kristen Carbone '02, and Kristina Podesva
for their assistance.

Ruins of a Sensibility, Nayland's installation featured on the
Tang Museum mezzanine, was the catalyst for several dance
parties throughout the fall of 2003 at Skidmore. Special thanks
to Gretchen Wagner, Tang Curatorial Assistant for organizing the
events, and to WSPN Skidmore College Radio board members
and many guest DJs who kept the piece spinning throughout
the semester; Brendon Boyle '05, Hannah Carlen '04, Pete Fox '04,
Kristina Ho '05, Helena Sanders '05, Jess Sauer '04, Ben Scheim
'04, Ezra Selove '04, Nikki Stewart '04, and Jocelyn Tunney '04.
Also thanks to Kristen Coates '05, Zaria Forman '05, Rosie
Garschina '03, Will Huessy '07, and John Suvannavejh '03 for
their regular DJing.

My sincerest thanks and affection go to Nayland Blake who
has touched so many during the course of
this exhibition. His lectures and informal
meetings with students and visitors both
at Skidmore and at UMBC were transfor-
mative moments for many. Nayland is
an inspirational teacher whose images
and words will remain with us for many
years to come.

—IAN BERRY, Curator

Ruins of a Sensibility
1972–2002, 2002
DJ equipment, records, wood,
cardboard boxes, painting
Installation view, Tang
Museum, Skidmore College

This catalogue accompanies the exhibition

NAYLAND BLAKE: *SOME KIND OF LOVE*
PERFORMANCE VIDEO 1989-2002

Center for Art and Visual Culture, University of Maryland, Baltimore County
February 6 – March 22, 2003

The Tang Teaching Museum and Art Gallery at Skidmore College
Saratoga Springs, New York
October 18, 2003 – January 4, 2004

The Tang Teaching Museum and Art Gallery
Skidmore College
815 North Broadway
Saratoga Springs, New York 12866
T 518 580 8080
F 518 580 5069
www.skidmore.edu/tang

This exhibition and publication are made possible in part with public funds from
the New York State Council on the Arts, a state agency, and the Friends of the Tang.

ISBN 0-9708790-9-1
Library of Congress control number: 2003101771

Front Cover:
Feeder 2, 1998
Gingerbread, steel
84 x 120 x 84"
Collections of Eileen Harris-Norton
and Peter Norton, Santa Monica

Page 1: *Bunny Bread* wrapper (detail)
Collection of Nayland Blake

Photographs:
Pages 21, 62–63, 74: Oren Slor
Page 25: John Berens
Page 31: Bill Jacobson
Page 73: Wolfgang Gunzel

Back Cover:
Heavenly Bunny Suit, 1994
Nylon, metal armature
72 x 35 x 19"
Courtesy of the artist and
Matthew Marks Gallery

Designed by Bethany Johns / Printed in Germany by Cantz